Hampstead, "an amiable, elevated lubberland, affording to London the example of a kind of surburban Nirvana"
Wilkie Collins 1824-89.

Heath Street and Baptist Church in 1906. Inset, as it is today.

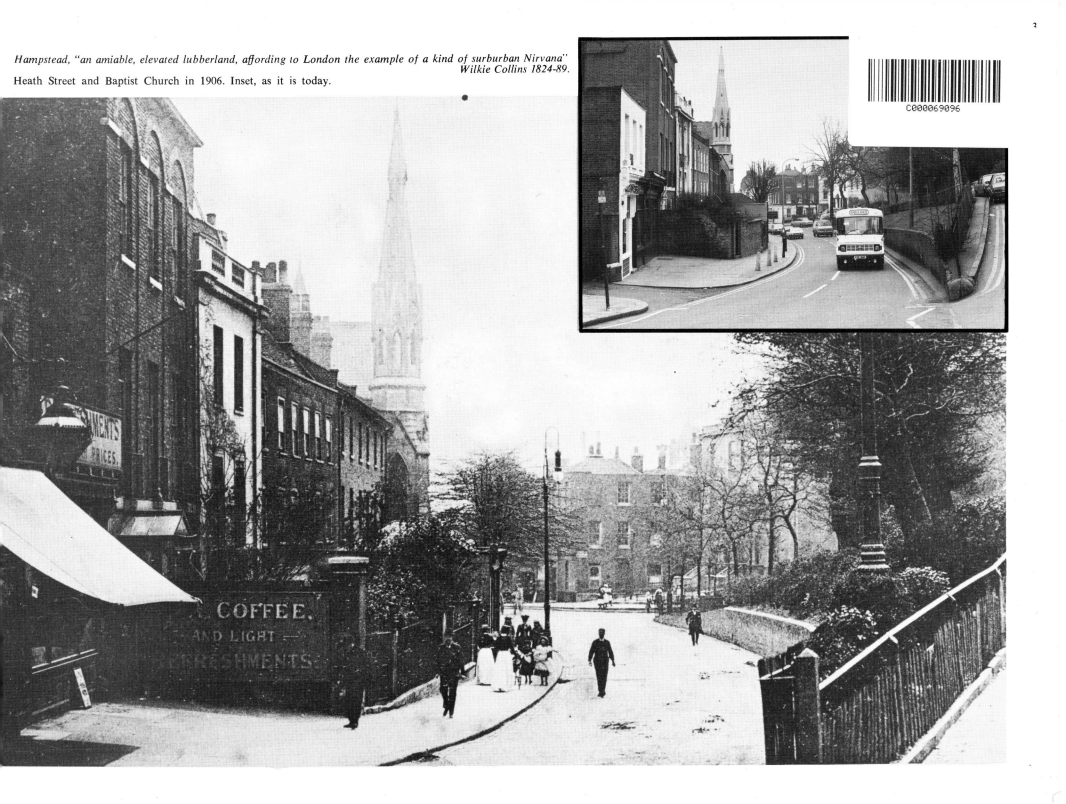

4

Flask Walk at the Well Walk end, 1905. The building on the right was the Flask Walk Baths and Laundry, built by the Wells and Campden Trust in 1888 to encourage cleanliness. It is now being converted into two houses, see inset.
*Well Walk and Flask Walk recall the fashionable spa of the 18th century.

High Street from Greenhill looking towards Holly Hill in 1906. Inset, as it is today.

Below and left: The High Street looking towards the old Hampstead Fire Station complete with watch-tower—now occupied by Nationwide Building Society. The fire station built in 1873 was number 14 in the Metropolitan Fire Brigade. The station closed during the first World War and was replaced by a new building in Lancaster Grove in 1915. The horse-bus in the picture below is near the Bird in Hand c. 1905. Inset, right, High Street as it is today.

Below: The High Street looking towards Rosslyn Hill, 1905. The King of Bohemia is on the left. A horse-bus is struggling up the hill. Note the third horse that was added to the team to help on the long pull up from Chalk Farm.

The church tower centre of picture, was part of the Trinity Presbyterian Church; built in 1862 it was demolished in 1962.

Inset, right, as it is today. The King of Bohemia, on left, was rebuilt in 1935. High Hill Bookshop can be seen centre of picture.

Church Row, looking towards the parish church of St. John 1906. This is a classic example of the old adage that a picture can say more than a thousand words. A delightful road of Georgian houses, dating from about 1720. The church of St. John was rebuilt entirely in 1745-7 from designs by John Sanderson. Many notable people are buried in its church yard, including John Constable.
Inset, as it is today. Thankfully very little change, apart from the parked cars and the absence of maids cleaning the doorsteps.

Rosslyn Hill, looking up the hill towards the High Street in 1905. The man walking in the road is mercifully unaware of the vast amount of motor traffic to come in later years. Inset, left: Lyndhurst Road Congregational Church, erected in 1883. The architect was Alfred Waterhouse.

Left: Prince of Wales Road, off Haverstock Hill, 1907.
Below, left: Haverstock Hill looking towards Hampstead Green and St. Stephen's Church.
Below: Passengers boarding a horse-bus outside St. Stephen's. The church dates from 1870. It is in French Gothic style, built of purple Luton bricks with granite and stone dressings. The architect was Samuel Sanders Teulon. In recent years the church has been closed because of structural problems. There have been various attempts to find a new use for the building, but its size and the enormous cost of repairs is a major problem. The Victorian Society are very concerned about this building.

Haverstock Hill N. W.
(shewing St. Stephen's Church).

WOMEN FIGHT AT FASCIST MEETING

Police Cordons: Four Arrests

HAND-TO-HAND fighting broke out in Hampstead Town Hall, N.W., last night, during a Fascist meeting. Ten men and two women were ejected.

Later four people were arrested and charged—two with using insulting words and behaviour, one with assaulting a police officer, and one with obstructing the police.

They will appear at Marylebone Police Court to-day.

The trouble started during a speech by Mr. William Joyce, director of propaganda of the British Union of Fascists, who was frequently heckled.

Much of the disorder broke out when Mr. Joyce attacked the Jews.

Some women were involved in a scuffle, and several exchanged blows.

Pandemonium broke out when the stewards were called upon to eject a woman interrupter.

Chairs were overturned, men and women were struggling on the floor, and the rest of the audience were shouting and screaming.

Further disorder broke out when the Fascists marched away to their local headquarters.

They were surrounded by a crowd yelling, "Down with the Black Rats!" Foot and mounted police were soon on the scene, and cordons were thrown across the road near the Fascist headquarters.

Haverstock Hill, 1907. The old Hampstead Town Hall, built in 1877, was the scene of many stormy council meetings and political gatherings. Perhaps the fiercest was the one reported in this clipping from the Daily Herald of October 23rd, 1938. On the outbreak of the Second World War, William Joyce went to Germany and regularly broadcast propaganda to Britain, being known as "Lord Haw Haw". He was tried for treason in 1945 and hanged. Inset, as it is today. Since the amalgamation of Hampstead with Holborn and St. Pancras into the new London Borough of Camden the building is no longer used for council meetings. The council's Engineering and Works Departments are now housed here.

Above left: Hampstead General Hospital as it was in 1906. It was replaced by the Royal Free Hospital, see picture above right. The new Royal Free admitted its first patients in October 1974.
Left: New End Hospital, 1915. And, above, as it is today.

This busy scene shows South End Road from South End Green, near the junction with Pond Street, 1906. Inset, as it is today.

Kite flying on Parliament Hill Fields, 1905.
Below: Parliament Hill as it was in 1908. And right, as it is today.
*Parliament Hill Fields, covering 267 acres, belonged mainly to the 4th Earl of Mansfield and was purchased in 1884-5 for £302,000.

Vale of Health, 1907.

Promenading along the Spaniards Road. This delightful picture was taken on a Sunday morning in 1920. Inset, the swings of Hampstead Heath fun-fair, 1910.

SWINGS, HAMPSTEAD HEATH.
ING TO TOUCH THE TREES"

The Spaniards Inn on the boundary of Hampstead. It is, in fact, just in the borough of Barnet. However, this celebrated inn and its associations with the famous—Dickens, Reynolds, Keats, Shelley, etc.—and the infamous Dick Turpin, is very much part of Hampstead history. Photo. 1907. Inset, as it is today.
*The building dates from 1585 and is believed to have been erected for a Spanish Ambassador at the time of James I.

Jack Straw's Castle as it was in 1907. Near the summit of the Heath, 440ft. above sea level. The inn dates back to at least 1713. Legend has it that Jack Straw, one of Wat Tyler's men in the peasants' revolt in 1381, met with his followers at this point.
The building was badly damaged by German Landmines during air attacks in 1940-41. It was completely rebuilt in 1962. See inset, right.

Above and below: Whitestone Pond, originally a horse pond. It must have been a welcome sight for horses after they had struggled up hill.

Above and below: Hampstead's first cinema—Biddalls Electric Show. It was one of the attractions at the fun-fair on the Heath in 1905.

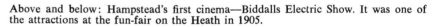

PPY 'AMPSTEAD. All the fun of the fair for the traditional Cockney celebrations on a Bank Holiday. Above, a barrel gan provides music for dancers. Right, Knees up Mother Brown to the strains of a mouth organ, 1902. Below, right: nny whelk stalls. Left: Flower seller from a contemporary drawing by Phil May.

*For the first wartime fair in 1940, the usual blare of music from the roundabouts, etc., was toned down. Council inspectors were there to ensure that any air raid warning would be heard.

AT 'APPY 'AMPSTEAD ON EASTER MONDAY.

PENNY A PLATE HAMPSTEAD HEATH

Florrie Forde, 1907.

"DOWN AT THE OLD BULL AND BUSH."

Come, come, come and make eyes at me,
  Down at the old Bull and Bush;
Come, come, drink some port wine with me,
  Down at the Old Bull and Bush.
Hear the little German Band,
Just let me hold your hand, dear,
Do, do come and have a drink or two,
  Down at the old Bull and Bush (Bush Bush).

NORTH END. The Bull and Bush. Made famous by t
popular music hall song. Down at the old Bull and Bus
see illustration, centre, from an Edwardian postca
Florrie Forde, music hall comedienne popularised t
Bull and Bush song. It was once said, when Flor
Forde sang a chorus number it was 'made'. She sa
Down at the old Bull and Bush—and the rest of us ha
sung it with gusto ever since.

Telephone : 1685 P.O. Hampstea

SPECIAL
2/-
ORDINARY

Every Sunday, 2 till 3.

Soups, Fish, Joints and
Poultry.
Sweets.   Vegetables
Cheese and Celery.
Roll and Butter

PRIVATE SITTING ROOMS TO ACCOMMODATE
SMALL AND LARGE PARTIES.

DINNER & TEA PARTIES
CATERED FOR.

The Bull and Bush as it was in 1921, showing the entrance to its terrace gardens, now sadly a car-park. Inset, as it is today.

NORTH END. Above: the Hare and Hounds in 1908. This building was destroyed by German bombs during air attacks in 1940. After a temporary building was used for many years, it was rebuilt in 1966. Left: Wyldes Farm, as it was in 1902. The old farmhouse is on the boundary of Hampstead. Charles Dickens made his first recorded visit to Hampstead here in 1837. Right: North End near the entrance to Golders Hill, 1905. Ivy House, with the tall chimneys, was the home of the famous ballerina, Anna Pavlova, above right. She lived here from 1912 until her death in 1931.

Wyldes Farm, as it was in 1902

Entrance to Golders Hill, Hampstead Heath.

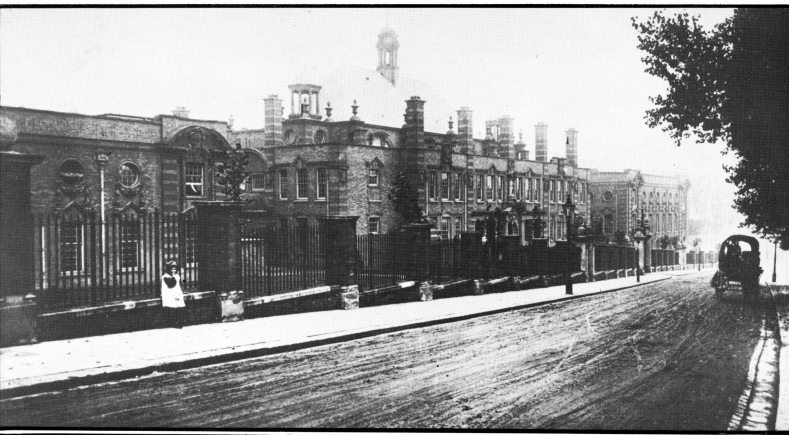

FROGNAL. Right: University College School in 1911. The school moved from Gower Street, when the new building was opened by King Edward VII on July 26th, 1907. Above.
Below, left: Frognal Lane looking towards the Finchley Road, 1908.
Below, right: Mill Lane, West Hampstead, 1905.

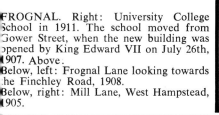

Fitzjohns Avenue, near the junction with College Crescent, 1906. Inset, as it is today.
*Between 1851 and 1900 the population of Hampstead rose from 12,000 to 80,000 and many new roads were con structed. In 1875, Fitzjohns Avenue was planned to form a link from Finchley Road to the village. The new roa ran across farmland.

England's Lane, near the junction with Primrose Hill Road. Inset, as it is today.

Belsize Park Gardens, 1911.

Above: Eton Avenue, 1912.

Right: Eton Avenue, 1912. The building on the left was then the Hampstead Conservatoire whose principal for many years was Cecil Sharp, founder of the English Folk Dance Society. It is now the Central School of Speech and Drama.
Below,: as it is today.

Finchley Road, near the Finchley Road Station, 1903. The station was rebuilt in 1939. Inset, as it is today. The Metropolitan line, opened in June 1879, was joined by the Bakerloo line in November 1939. This then became part of the new Jubilee line on May 1st, 1979.

Fellows Road South Hampstead N. W.

Above, left: Church of St. Mary the Virgin, Primrose Hill, 1907. Built in 1871-5 from designs of M. P. Manning.

Above, right: Fellows Road, South Hampstead, 1907.

Right: All Hallows Church in Savernake Road, Gospel Oak, 1905. All Hallows, built of Kentish ragstone, mainly designed by the well-known Victorian architect James Brooks. The foundation stone is dated 1892. The dedication of the Church was the result of the sale of site of All Hallows, Great Thames Street, in the City, which helped to finance the new All Hallows, Gospel Oak. The money was insufficient to complete the church to Brooks' original design, and he died in 1901. Internally, the vaulting which he had planned was not completed until 1913, being designed by Sir Giles Gilbert Scott. In spite of its interrupted design and erection, the interior is particularly dignified.

All Hallows Church & Savernake Road, Hampstead N. W.

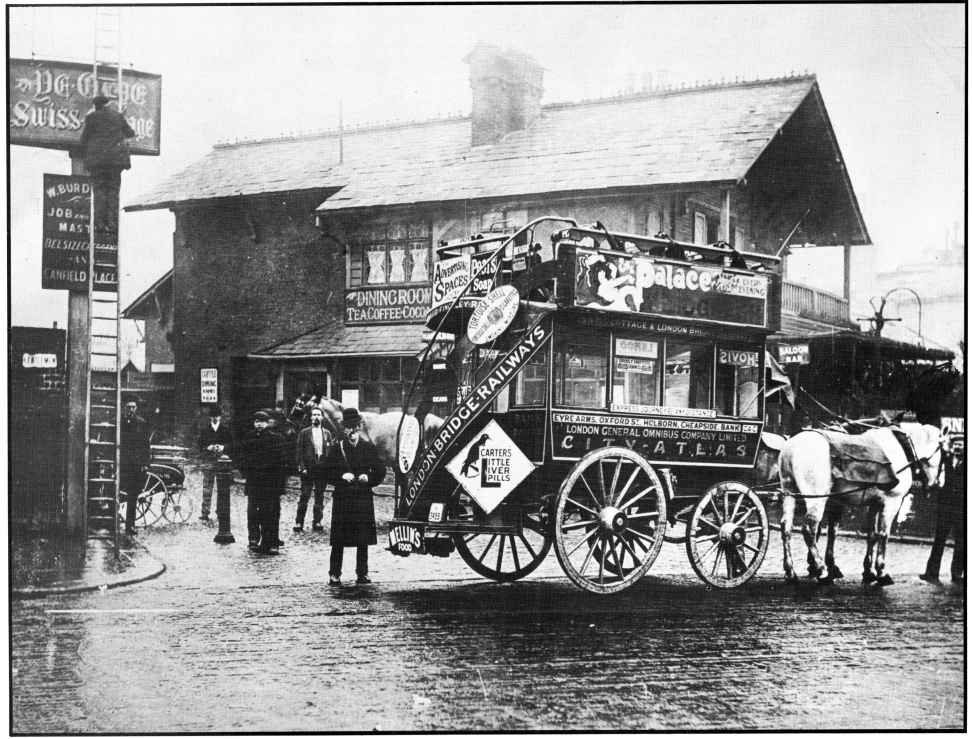

Changing horses at Swiss Cottage, 1902. One of the "express" buses which ran from Swiss Cottage to the Bank. A flat fare of 6d was charged for any distance.

Keats House as it was in 1910—then known as Lawn Bank. The house dates from 1815-16. It was here in the spring of 1819 that John Keats wrote Ode to a Nightingale. In 1920 the house was put up for sale and a campaign was launched to purchase it as a memorial to Keats. The £10,000 was raised with more than £2,500 coming from the United States. The house was first opened to the public in 1925.

Kenwood House, Highgate, is believed to date from 1710. It was sold by Lord Bute to William Murray who later became Earl of Mansfield. With Robert Adam as architect, he began to enlarge the house in 1767. The Mansfield family retained ownership until in 1924 the 4th Earl sold the house and ground to Lord Iveagh. The house, its collection of paintings and furniture, plus 89 acres of grounds were bequeathed to the public by Lord Iveagh on his death in 1927. Photo. 1928.

Burgh House, New End Square. Built in 1703. William Gibbons, physician, lived here in 1720 and his initials still grace its wrought-iron gates. In 1858 it was taken over by the Royal East Middlesex Militia. A more recent tenant was Elsie Bambridge, Rudyard Kipling's daughter. Kipling's last outing before his death in 1936 was to Burgh House. After surviving the bombs of the Second World War, the house was bought by Hampstead Borough Council in 1947. In 1977 the building was threatened by dry rot. Residents formed a Burgh House Trust and raised £50,000. The house was restored by Camden Council, leased to the Trust and opened to the public in 1979 as a meeting place, exhibition centre and museum.

THE HAMPSTEAD TUBE

A company formed in 1893 to build a tube railway from Charing Cross to Heath Street failed to raise sufficient money. When American financier Charles Tyson Yerkes bought the rights in 1900 for £100,000 he secured the backing of other wealthy Americans to the extent of £30,000,000. His experience of American railways and the possibilities of opening up new areas led him to change the terminus from Heath Street to the open spaces of Golders Green. The tunnels between Hampstead and Golders Green were started from both ends and when they met at a point about 100 yards north of Heath Street the error was only three quarters of an inch! At Heath Street the railway lines are almost 200 feet below ground. The new tube line was opened in June 1907, when the first train was started by David Lloyd George, then President of the Board of Trade. Travel was free that day and 140,000 people took advantage of this.

Heath Street Station, 1909.